Let's Explore Gases

by Anne J. Spaight

BUMBA BOOKS™

LERNER PUBLICATIONS ◆ MINNEAPOLIS

Note to Educators:

Throughout this book, you'll find critical thinking questions. These can be used to engage young readers in thinking critically about the topic and in using the text and photos to do so.

Lerner Publications Company
A division of Lerner Publishing Group, Inc.
241 First Avenue North
Minneapolis, MN 55401 USA

For reading levels and more information, look up this title at www.lernerbooks.com.

Library of Congress Cataloging-in-Publication Data

Names: Spaight, Anne J., 1983– author.
Title: Let's explore gases / by Anne J. Spaight.
Description: Minneapolis : Lerner Publications, [2018] | Series: Bumba books.
  A first look at physical science | Audience: Ages 4–7. | Audience: K to Grade 3.
  | Includes bibliographical references and index.
Identifiers: LCCN 2017024977 (print) | LCCN 2017019803 (ebook) | ISBN
  9781512482720 (eb pdf) | ISBN 9781512482683 (lb : alk. paper) | ISBN
  9781541510814 (pb : alk. paper)
Subjects: LCSH: Gases—Properties—Juvenile literature. |
  Matter—Properties—Juvenile literature.
Classification: LCC QC161.2 (print) | LCC QC161.2 .S67 2018 (ebook) | DDC
  530.4/3—dc23

LC record available at https://lccn.loc.gov/2017024977

Manufactured in the United States of America
1 – CG – 12/31/17

LERNER
e
SOURCE

Expand learning beyond the printed book. Download free, complementary educational resources for this book from our website, www.lerneresource.com.

Table of
Contents

What Are Gases?

Matter is everything around us.

Gases are one type of matter.

You cannot see most gases.

The air is made of gases.

We can see things that float

in gases.

Tiny water drops float

in gas.

This makes fog and clouds.

You can feel gases.

Feel the wind.

See it blow in the trees.

Gases are in the wind. What are some things the wind helps us do?

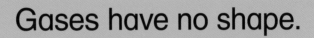

Gases have no shape.

They spread to fill

a container.

They escape if there

is no lid.

Helium is a gas.

We use it to fill balloons.

Helium makes balloons float.

13

We blow bubbles.

Bubbles are gas trapped in a liquid.

What other liquids can you blow bubbles into?

15

Liquid boils into steam.

Steam is water vapor with

water drops floating in it.

Water vapor cannot be seen.

Water drops form on the outside

of a cold glass.

This is water vapor turning into liquid.

When have you seen water drops on a glass? Was it hot or cold outside?

Breathe in and breathe out.

Gases are everywhere.

Picture Quiz

Which of these pictures show gases?

Picture Glossary

boils

makes bubbles of vapor when heated

fog

water vapor suspended in the air low to the ground

matter

something that takes up space, or has weight

vapor

a type of gas

Read More

Hanson-Harding, Alexandra. *What Is Matter?* New York: Britannica Educational Publishing, 2015.

Hoffmann, Sara E. *Gases*. Minneapolis: Lerner Publications, 2013.

Midthun, Joseph. *Matter and How It Changes*. Chicago: World Book, 2012.

Index

Photo Credits

The images in this book are used with the permission of: © Leena Robinson/Shutterstock.com, pp. 5, 23 (bottom left); © Milosz_G/Shutterstock.com, pp. 6–7, 23 (top right); © Robert Kneschke/Shutterstock.com, pp. 8–9; © Michal Ludwiczak/Shutterstock.com, pp. 10–11; © kali9/iStock.com, p. 13; © Patrick Foto/Shutterstock.com, pp. 14–15; © Kei Shooting/Shutterstock.com, pp. 17, 23 (top left); © Nickeline/Shutterstock.com, pp. 18, 23 (bottom right); © mangostock/Shutterstock.com, pp. 20–21; © Nenov Brothers Images/Shutterstock.com, p. 22 (top left); © Toa55/Shutterstock.com, p. 22 (top right); © pashyksvsv/Shutterstock.com, p. 22 (bottom left); © Country Lane Studios/Shutterstock.com, p. 22 (bottom right).

Front Cover: © yuris/Shutterstock.com.